Wellspring

poems by

Sarah Stemp

Finishing Line Press
Georgetown, Kentucky

Wellspring

ACKNOWLEDGMENTS

"Friend of My Mind" has been published in *New Reader, 5:19*

Publisher: Leah Huete de Maines
Editor: Christen Kincaid
Cover Art: Mary Pond
Author Photo: Sarah Stemp
Cover Design: Elizabeth Maines McCleavy

Order online: www.finishinglinepress.com
also available on amazon.com

Author inquiries and mail orders:
Finishing Line Press
PO Box 1626
Georgetown, Kentucky 40324
USA

Contents

Wellspring—

1. the source of a stream, spring; fountainhead
2. a source of abundant and continual supply

Morning Walk with Emily D.

1.
The morning walk, framed. *My business is circumference.*
Difference set in bounds. The road itself
is bounded, set against. Oak and elm on each side arching, concealing
and revealing blue or white sky, distant hills. Flipped on their backs,
the leaves are silver. Which side silver, which side silk.

2.
Circumscription enables Wo
—were not limit—Who
were sufficient to Misery?
Were it not for boundary, who among us could bear?
The path is form itself, and its *internal differences, where*
the Meanings are: the bent bough, the crooked and half-cracked.

3.
Dear Friend, I felt it shelter to speak to you. Housed
in perimeter, safely hemmed, yet Errant
sticking-out-sideways. Willful, whorled—*myself the only kangaroo*
among the Beauty—
but master, I'm *Alive.*
You may be the holder of words, even so I am
Speaker.

4.
Naming: grayish or milky fog or mist rising,
two dead trees dignified and standing,
then layers of low ground and open meadow and mounds
of manure so rich it can't keep from blooming.
At the seam of the road, clover and many small daisies.

5.
Walking limns motions of mind, syntax, &
cadence, a Slant self-sounding. Am I shut-in
if I still can sing?
The smallest sprinkle of buttercup

stands up and is Rendered. On one side, dashes,
patches of sunlight on the forest floor, and suddenly
brambles bearing tiny clusters of purple grapes.

6.

The loudest difference is Shadow. Weaver of exaggerate
shape, caller to Account. Under the spruce's fullness
crowned reflection darkens. Pattern spreads, vibrates.
It's the line that makes the thing.

7.

I, beset all-around by circumspection: Run amok, *Awe*
serves no one. Possessed by Shelter, a tamed thaw—
compressed, folded, & sewed. Whose order
is shut inside the structure of a sentence?
Am I shut-in?

8.

On the road, the edges are how things show themselves—
trench and furrow, stripe of goldenrod, swath of hyssop
against the wide grass. Relations of opposition
depend on light—the low growth in shadow,
the tops lit, and wet.

9.

Circumference, the verge of meaning's confine:
On a dewey morning, to reveal is to encircle, but also to loose—
what appear to be webs of water woven placed or resting
atop the long grass, silvery and shining.

10.

The pond, a vessel, with rims and a skirt.
Rounded with spruce, full of deep-sky reflection—
wide bowl of white and blue, waiting.
One could easily fall from its ledge dropping down and down dizzied,
uncurtailed.

11.
My mother does not care for thought. Could you tell me
what home is? I never had a mother.
Circumference: that Region where imagination comes into play,
where mind is Borne—the mother's mind, wherein the child may
sojourn, and come to be able to be.

12.
Walking uphill, this rise, that fall. Were it not
for these, all would be void, unmade.
If *Blank*, a circle could not be. Without circumference
the circle neither is nor means.

13.
Open closed open. Blank becomes delineated,
worlded. Trees turn. Cows chew, crows call,
worms inch and wind moves.
Call these by name so as not to bereave.
This path—a hermit's devotion. A belonging.
If I sing, am I a shut-in?

14.
Though I am bridled of mind, I am not bereaved.
Circumference does not kill light
or the low rub of cicadas or birdsong.
This deference to form contents me. It's a solace
and a spell.

15.
Early autumn brings a rampant tinge.
I thought when the trees' descent began, the light would leave.
Even so, time turns—early
goldenrod harbinger of a vast yellow leafing,
thickets tameless and showy, even
as far as magenta.

16.
October on the path, I am all respect.
The trees still bound your margins. Your patience
has been, against chaos, a home.
The green velvet sack in which you have sheathed
me is returning to an older brown, crumpled rust
and dusty yellow.

17.
We are now in the district of disintegration.
Your charmed structure protects.
I walk and watch the light transfusions
and all the russet weeds, the reddened reedy hay,
the sweeping skirts of branches, bared.
Still, you keep the world intact. It is
the form of you I set my heart on.

Parts of Speech: Elegy for My Mother

For she was a hoarder of her own heart, for
all was a tenderness too far.

Let shadows be a weight and cool.
Let consolation austere.
Let the severe way of things.
Pray for ice, planed and polished. Pray for
the shut heart.
Wherefrom fall the shadows and the shut?
From sorrow like ice, like old moss, old scars,
like strain.

Even the small plants open
their leaves, the milkmaids and the modesty
and the lady's smock, and the red sorrel which looks like a big clover.
I try to follow their roaring, but stop
at disresemblances. I am not lifted up.
I keep to myself such
ways of care as I am able.
I'm homesick for my heart, my tongue's first habits
of mind. Afflicted and various,
I am blocked from finding.

We did not grow round each other like vines.

Everything only connected by 'and' and 'and'—
an intimate grammar. Love
for the bodies of words.
You scored highest in the whole country on the Latin exam, *remorari...*
I look for your body—
and find it in the bodies of words. I finger
their jagged grains, their silky underparts:
Gold, rust, rose, blood, milk.
Aurum, rusticum, roseus, sanguinem, lacte.

Stuck to you through parts of speech, searching for blood.
Your least instruction a tenderness too far.

5

Friend of My Mind

You, a tree, in me,
over time.
If it dread, if it darken, if fall
to ruin, you will do, this too,
the next thing…over time.
Now one foot now the other. Now
late, even. I am keeper of undermined,
you are patient.
All of us, any of us, you said, *I wasn't born*
this way.
I, unbuilt.
See how the thickening clouds yield light snow.
Why am I unseasonably cool?
Friend of my mind:
We restore ancient things, sweet, salt, &
bitter. We bring things back and back.
The dark is big.
I met you in the district of rain, the tears
of things. Later than we might have known,
but both still vivid.
I am in the habit of you, and sometimes
able to, my soft parts, tenderly.
Things that have to do with enlargement.
What had been required of you.
If I had not submitted, nowhere.
Also, what you yourself went through affects
interpenetration:
We investigate each other's bearings.
Things come up between us, wide.
I am glad this journey with you, you said.
Sometimes, with you, I luminate.
Abiding.

Virus-time: Consolations

1. Between the concrete side and the rope

Held up against the side, hard unmoving
blue. Rely utterly on, fasten on, framed,
saved. Covenant—
weight of wall and weight of water.
Consolation corridor.

The water itself solid, itself
heavy, scooped, cupped.
Pressing, pulling,
pumping power.
In my lane, chlorine kills,
protects, succors.

Hard body moves between
bright blue lines, marked, comprised
of small square tiles, aligned,
secured.
Locked in certainty,
a concrete vow.

2. Form/No-form

How our orders have been messed with.
How mighty form has fallen
        unleashed and swarming.
How old hurts have opened, and I am again
        early, back with no recourse, at
        mercy of. Back in the old form,
        not of my making.
How to make new, now, amidst a million losses.
Here are the gestures of my hands.

3. In the country: Fall, 2020

Dump of green gone
to air, to seed and dust, drying
into color and dust, leaving
hard plain form.
Leaves lost in wet smell of yellow
and mud, leaving only
lines in the light,
clean
and terribly clear.

Against the sky, a branch has parts.
Dividing, a fine thinning to twig.
Grey/brown/black, dark grain
mottled to filament. No green.
A certain austere arrangement, not a leafing.
The motions of the mind of the branch are
calm. Engaged with its own formal sufficiency, nothing
prevents it from practicing its inwardness,
the order it makes, and feels.

I am all regard:
Your restriction, itself a wideness.
Your fine-grained and finite features, patient
in the rain-soaked air
in the sodden sun.
My beholding serving your poised particulars—
how each twig divides further and finer
and the light around you thickens and lightens and
moves your weight towards
me. Unworried, sparely your form
composes. Holding the sun along your length,
holding your own consecrated weight.
You are of sanctifying use.
All morning you have been branching,
unstudied, and merely shining.

4. The therapist returns to her office in the city,
after a year-and-a-half in the country

I dropped down and kissed
the floor. Beloved ground, holder
of a million griefs.
Blue and rust rug, leather
chairs, like earth. Controlled
air, color, silence. Long
soft couch against the wall, weight
of memories of bodies come with memories.
After great pain, formal
home of my making.
Unforsaken
place of beauty, strain.
Snarl of muddle, haunting, unforeseen
ranting, sudden floods.
Looseness unruly, holy melding, holy
mess.
Sack of transgression and test. Box
of bedlam. Our rim
nearly overrun, but still
holding.
Danger in gestures in
corners in doors in
holes and hallways,
held, still.

5. Inside the poem

You did not abandon us
formless, abyss of
darkness with no
face. *You rescue me from dispersal
and give me a sure shape*, gathered
ordered and called
sky, earth, human.

Does Form mean I can rest in it?
Our rest is our place.
Morning, evening.
Waters above, waters
below, and *a well under the waters
where the Muse moves.*

Line upon line, *a stay against*,
set against, a making—
even, uneven, a wave
leaving and coming and coming
to rest.
These incantatory orderings,
in the course of, Form occurs.
Underwater contours—
indigo, cobalt, azure, even periwinkle and
grey. Changes of light,
blue and hazy, dark green
and close-up.
Twining shapes, single tendril, wayward
branch.

Words, weights on the tongue, sounds
tested and plumbed. Tones
delicate, bitter, layered, lit.
Sculpture made of air
of strings of sound, of breath and hush.

In the wake of a poem,
a formed unraveling.
First home—a mother's mind. Mine, for a long season.
Labor made of her ruin and her hope.

What I heard in the first moment when I grieved for you...

Mother: your memories
become my treasure.
These things fill from behind, beneath,
from overturnedness
from ghosts.
House made of female rain:
House made of your Latin prizes,
later failures, songs:
> *when you followed followed me*
> *in that land you followed me*
> *land neither planted*
> *nor seeded*

Shelter her limits and my losses.

Form pinned down, lamentation
ordered in waves, in circles, in pleats.
I assume the writing position:
Mother, I have set something by for you:
The wrested ridge by which the horizon is seen.
A resting place between steep and flat,
against sorrow like smoke, like vapor—
a sure scarred shape
a hewed grave place.

Wellspring

1.
Having replaced the receiver in its cradle, attached
to the knotted cord of the old landline, his voice
no longer coming into my ear,
I sit in my chair in the maelstrom, in the wellspring, conceived.
—   Despite your fears that it will dry up, freeze up, close up,
          it is fed by an underground spring, come from your roaming
          and your patience, he said. Let it come. Let the form
          grow with faith in its own…
Comes suddenly to me—an image of an infant, attached
by the cord emerging from her mother's
navel—conception, creation through channel, another
making of art.
But wait—
the cord does not come
from the mother's center—it
comes through the open place.

How does something get born?
How does something get borne.
Tell me a birth story that is not about loss
and love.

2.

Athena emerges full-grown
from the head of Zeus, her father.
Armored thickly like a skull, something
hard.
Where does the hardness come from?
Here's what happened:
Zeus develops an erection, and needs
a home for his heat. Couldn't manage
to impregnate himself, so he nabs some
young seamstress named Metis, and sticks
in his stuck-out piece.
Dismay and a sense of doom foretold, followed by
post-coital hunger, he gulps the girl down, killing
two birds with one stone—a cover-up, and
hunger assuaged.

Meanwhile, Metis (raped, impregnated,
then swallowed with child by Zeus to prevent
offspring from overthrowing him) keeps her daughter company,
in the bowels of the father's body.

Time passes...

The young swallowed seamstress weaves
what she knows.
Her red rage feeds on itself and
grows—woven armor for her daughter
never to be made weak or woozy
never to be made a mother.
Her time served, her
sacrifice complete, the mother
leaves from the bottom-hole—a pile of
dung and discard. Leaving her daughter
motherless, still inside the godman.

Mother, you gave me armor
but not yourself.

3.
His low maternal voice
in my ear:
—   It's hard to trust that your own process
         will rebirth itself—endlessly emergent, like
         a wellspring.
Comes suddenly an image of myself as an older child lying
the length of my parents' bed, bodying forth
silent red welts.
The welts rose at the end of an afternoon, at the end of years
of serving as my father's muse and mirror, while
my mother mothered the others.
Now, as I told of how the welts rose requiring
my father's attention,
I heard the voice again
well up in my ear:
—   What comes out of you moves me, how your inside
         gathers, weaves, comes to be.
Wellspring, welts, welling up—
a writer weaving and shaping
a birthing
upthrusting and low-gathering,
unarmored and free.

4.

Inside the godman, Athena swims upstream, sperm-like,
and begins a wild kicking, inducing
an ache so unbearable
and head-splitting, that Zeus,
with the help of his hammer-wielding cronies,
breaks open his own brains, blasting
a bony channel to relieve himself:

Hard-armored, red-gold layered, woven
of all she has left of her dead mother,
Athena, ready, springs forth—
covered in brain sap,
sheathed, locked, and loaded.

5.

I was my father's favorite, the eldest,
his muse and his mirror. My mother,
neither strong nor free,
named flowers and read me poetry
but did not see me, leaving me
longing to be like the strut and
shine of my father's mind.

6.
A woman weaving armor
in the darkened belly of a god.
Light playing on the goldwork—
is it metal thread or gossamer?
Of what mettle the metallic fibers, reddish yarns
of plain weave, sheet warp and wire weft, many-
stranded thin wires twisted
together? Malleable but locking
in place, adding strength
and sound structure. While
the metal is soft enough to weave, does it harden
in the weaving, and again, in the shaping?

A woman weaving armor.
A mother giving birth.
Metis, patient patroness of weaving and women's arts,
goddess of prudence, sacrifice, and care—
too womanish,
you bore a daughter responsible
for your own death.
You gave her sojourn and seed
of protection, but you
disappeared, subsumed. Your armor
not hard enough to save yourself,
you left your daughter motherless—requiring
a second birth.

Athena, twice born, of double sojourn and
gender queer—
freed from your mother's weak ways,
springing forth, erect and strong—
you become both daughter and son.

Weaponized and wise, Athena
identifies:
She vows to husband her own power—
hoard desire hereafter,
only for herself.
Swearing eternal chastity
free of gender and need
She-who-is-unto-herself comes to be
at full liberty
to birth her own agency.
Motherless childless goddess:
No one will rob rape or ram you.
No child will consume you.
Your father's thunderbolt will be—
your inheritance
and your legacy.

7.

Mother-man, I dreamt of you
last night:
I was minding my business, goddess of
my own assertions and exertions, when suddenly you
came over, though I
was still in view. We embraced, and somehow
came through
each whole, for me
something new.

Still, so much easier to have you
in my dream or your voice in my ear,
than to deal
with your real male body.
Remember that time long ago, when you bent over
me to adjust the heat—how fearfully,
ragefully, I responded?

But coming
through my ear, I
take you in:
Your warm voice gender-free, encouraging patient audacity
of birthing—
weaving, underwriting, overwriting—
a palimpsest, a personal way,
neither man-ish nor woman-ish, you say.
Let's call it self-ish, you say.
Power ungendered, full
of itself.

8.
In some versions of the story, Metis
is a Titan-goddess, source of
shrewdness, cunning and deep thought.
In fact, some say—
Zeus had no brains at all, until he swallowed his
wise wife.

What does it mean that Athena came out
of her father's head, if her intelligence
was from her mother?
With her brains and his power
the daughter cut form out of air
and weaponized it.

Did Metis engineer her daughter's escape, shrewdly
setting up the launching,
while Athena, honoring
her mother's hopes, made more of Metis
than she could make of herself—thus atoning
for the matricide, forgiving and redeeming
her mother's failing?

Whether Metis finally turned into Zeus's shit or his
brains, one thing is clear:
Athena, emancipated,
gave back to her mother a gift—becoming
what she was unable to be—
for Metis, a form of immortality.
But somewhere along the way
the grateful daughter birthing
herself full-grown and whole, smacking of
no childlike quality, no vulnerability,
betrays her mother's maternity,
rejecting eternity,
hardening in the shaping.
Weaving from both parents
an androgeny,
she vows
no progeny will be her legacy.
Forever-virgin goddess of Olympus,
childless,
of unimpeded mind
of undistracted mind
uninterrupted
unwaylaid
twice-born and many-gendered
Athena, issues forth.

9.
As for me, my children sown
hard and soft and grown
birthed in risk and trial
can the poet and the mother reconcile?

To husband my own mind, to hoard
my thoughts without thwartings and redirection
not interruption unto death, not
only to begin and begin and begin
in divided stolen time.
They say you have become
a recluse, solitary, isolate,
miserly and avaricious.
Mercy to my greed, I say.
To live a wide
inwardness, wellspring of my own
making.

My language hardening in the shaping,
woven of loose fragments found and made
armed with authority,
the poet bodies forth.

Foreclosed in Three Parts

Foreclosed #1

Trust me. I have it in the bag. The outcome is not uncertain.
The bag is closed. Let there be no commerce coming or going
through my open wounds.
Let scars foreclose.

All I need—bandaids, scotchtape, ziplocs,
are in the bag. Air pressed out. Shut in. Cinched.
Sufficient as long comfort packaged
for the long haul.

Back-up to the back-up, prepared, lest.
More than enough shampoo, tissues, toilet paper,
in case of. I'll get out in front of
anything. Early.

Your comings and goings overrun
my rims. Open yourself, you say to me, as you enter.
My margins cannot curb your measures. All of this,
I am at the mercy of.

Give me no sunshine. No open soaring.
No soft hungers.

Let me lean only on reliable walls.

Foreclosed #2

Stand guard lest the heart
be seduced. Forswear. Let
aesthetics of foreclosure please
more than pleasure.
Let me not return to the wreck
of my formative years.

The dump of things done to me. Let
self-sufficiency be. Let refusal
defuse the variability
of your patience, your uncertain
reliability, your inconstant
delivery.

Am I to try to practice trust?
Risk your failure to take responsibility, your shame
projected onto me? Forswear. Let foreclosure please
more than trust. The worst threat
is not loneliness.

Foreclosed #3

Air shaft outside my window, surrounding
an internal courtyard. I keep
the blinds down and leave
the slats slightly open.
Walled grey courtyard, reliably sunless
and hard.

Inside my room, all is
as it should be. Muted rusts, blues, olive-ochres, half-
lit. Veil hung, grey hung, in the balance
of my preferences and particularities. Protection from
all my losses.

Illumination foreclosed. No quandries
of clangor or striving.
I believe in foregone conclusions—forewarned
is forearmed is foretold. All I have
is this effort, this drawing down.
Let there be no occurrences.

What with dread, and no guarantees, all I have
is this devotion, a dull joy. All I have
is this devotion,
a seal on my heart, on the tears of
inward things.

My Mother's Desire

When I try to remember my mother's desire
I see only how she put sour cream
in her cold-cereal-and-milk.
Her piles of paper and all her rumpled recipes ripped
by my father's rages. She called herself
passive aggressive, referring to the piles.

Mom, now that you're dead, you have a second chance.

Now, in my womb (snug as a bug in a rug), you can become
revolutionary.
1949: Your senior thesis—
Aspects of strain in sex-roles of Harvard and Radcliffe undergraduates.
Young women mourning in advance
what they were about to give up—their minds.
On cue, you did it too. Gave up your mind,
gave it over to me, to house and to hold
till death do us part.

Did you groom me, sourly, ragefully, to become
your mother? No one, now, will eat your heart
or rob your good brain.
Your motherless child will preserve protect contain.

But did I do the same?

Did I do the same? On cue, I too
bore children, less in number, full measure
of joy and pain. And my mind, split,
desire divided—
work of meaning, work of raising,
disordered eating, and mourning,
to house and to hold
while the day declines.

Dream Sequence

Dream #1

Upon rising to go to the bathroom:

A basement with two stalls. In each, a toilet-full of shit.
Inside a third, a naked woman dancer, stands
on a shelf.
First, the shit: Big elongated globs—time
with my fat father in his bathroom, with his big torpedos.
Then, the surprising woman: upright, on one foot
then the other, slowly
shifting weight, arms reaching, first one, then the other,
in thrall.
Who is she, unperturbed
next to all that shit?
Tall, on a calm flat shelf. Surprisingly
alive.

Two-thirds clogged up. But next door,
the woman, in love with herself. In love
with what it's like to send out length through limbs,
the slow feel of her own thrall.
A silence about her. Will there be more?
Not looking up at the one who opens the door.

She lives inside, aside, alone, protected by a wall,
supported by a shelf.
More than a thing of beauty, she is no
statue. She moves only for herself, as if before
her own mirror. Not of service, does not
want to share.

Dream #2

She hates the word *open*, especially
when it's spoken slowly.
But lying on her side, in the dream, she is with a woman.
The woman gently opens her and says over
and over, but you're so open, open. And
somehow she is able to stay
just there. Red, the woman says, you are
read, she says, staring.
And the poet just stays, letting it go
on and on.

Dream #3

To be with you I have to
block you out. But
could it be the point is not
to find a way around fear?
Welcome, welcome: Fear has soft
skin and warm hollows under her arms
and at the very bottom of her back.
How sufficient she is.
Her eyes are closed, her eyelids
satin, the lashes cornsilk.
She appreciates the blue and silver carpet laid out
in her honor.
She is surprised by this patience
and absence of unease.

There will be
no speaking. Only an unconveyed
but encouraged weaving.
A blush spreads over things.
She slowly shows her
velvet underbelly, and makes
a small sigh.

Dream #4

First, Second, and Third Sorrowful Mysteries:

First, why does she want to show
Herself? To proclaim her steely
Colors dark as plums, bright
As too much light.
She wants to feel them
Looking.

Second, how can she work
With what she has? Will it gather and weave? When do
Pieces of particular grief become fit for
Use.

Third, will unduly
Slender wrists and forearms be
Enough to lift?
Still the weight is heavy, the hour
Low and late.

Dream #5

Interior.
Despite baggy structure, plain, dismally
shy, let it.
Unpressed time, doesn't have to.
A kind of limitedness, undignified, this too.
All coming from small far suffering places, our
only partial turns from grief.
Measure will pick up insufficiency, inhibition—
now we're getting into judgement
and turning of the screws.
Give me let-down and non-performance, and small
soft sloping, mere feeling of.

Dream #6

My small folds veiled.
Refined. Seams severely,
neatly, stitched.
Comes Patience, a surprising suitor, a person surely
not worried about not being normal. A person of no
pressure who is not suffused by.
Wellspring of no necessity.
Like some way
that allows for.

But without need, how can a thing get
made? A world open out or a seam
unfurl?
How can patience
have no desire?
A dream.

Dream #7

On a roll, quietly, in the area of concern.
Enough to catch onto
an inside current, riding.
Patience enters,
dressed in pale rose, smelling her
way forward, trailing some gauzy
light thing, behind.
She wanders, with no standards, sounding.
We stroll, loll and lounge about,
smelling around.

Don't you tell me
magnanimously,
that whatever I decide is up to me.
It's not for you to say. Certainly,
it's up to me.

You can walk behind us, carrying the gossamer train of her gown.

Reading *Lila* by Marilynne Robinson

Anything come back to life, has to hurt
To touch shame with even the balm of
dignity, has to hurt

You were a shy child
Your thin arms and open face and bowed legs (that made it hard
for you to excel at running, you were always picked next-to-last
when it came to choosing teams)
Your short stature and your oval pale-blue
plastic glasses diminishing
your deep-set eyes, your heavy brown bangs,
your well-spoken grandmother said obscured
your intelligent brow, Why don't you show off
your brow?

You were not *left weltering*
in your blood
You were not *cast out in an open field*
Your person was not *abhorred*
You were brought close embraced secured
inside your warm house

Still you were left weltering.
No eye saw you
except his, not a seeing:
you, impaled by his strutting, staring
his face force-field of radiance coming at you, barreling
his face, soaked in light, at you, blazing
only seeing him, no eye saw you

What is a body to do to gain footing fill out feel out gain
foothold gain traction find
traces?

And how would a girl like that
make any kind of life, asking more of her than watching?

Ate him up with her eyes
worked herself up and spent it all on him
nothing left to start something
nothing left to seed

She would have needed a noticing or a ruthlessness.
One hadn't happened, and the other was waiting on a
girl who couldn't yet bother
about her own astonishment,
a girl whose own flaunting
held no appeal

What am I that you are mindful of me?
I am a likeness of scratched things
I am an ember of pride to be
enlarged
There is no problem so great as the shame of it,
said one psychoanalyst.
And another said, after I sang to him,
If I may, he said, plain
as day, You have a good voice.
I'll reflect on it, I said, as the salve made room,
I wouldn't mind if the shaming died down a little,
as the salve made room for more
ragtag life.

Notes

The definition of *wellspring* in the epigraph is taken from Webster's New World College Dictionary, fourth edition.

In *Morning Walk with Emily D.*, all italicized lines are direct quotes from the poems or letters of Emily Dickinson.

Everything only connected by 'and' and 'and', in *Parts of Speech: Elegy for My Mother*, is from Elisabeth Bishop's *Over 2,000 Illustrations and a Complete Concordance*.

The section in *Friend of My Mind* that begins *If it dread, if it darken…* is refracted from Lucie Brock-Broido's poem *Everything Husk to the Will*. The phrase, *friend of my mind*, is from *Beloved*, by Toni Morrison.

In *Virus-time: Consolations*, the line *Here are the gestures of my hands*, is from Jane Kenyon's *Year Day*. The lines *You rescue me from dispersal and give me sure shape*, and *Our rest is our place*, come from St Augustine's *Confessions*. *A well under the waters where the Muse moves*, is paraphrased from Denise Levertov's *The Illustration—A Footnote*. The phrase, *House of female rain* is taken from the Navajo night-chant, *House Made of Dawn*.

In *Reading "Lila", by Marilynne Robinson*, the italicized phrases are quotes from *Lila*, and some are refracted from the Bible (Psalms, Ezekiel).

***

This collection is dedicated to Jane Lazarre:
beloved teacher, splendid writer, brave and wise friend.

Friend of My Mind is for Tom Menaker.

Sarah Stemp is a poet and psychologist/psychoanalyst in New York City and has published poems in *New Reader* and *Psychoanalytic Perspectives*. She is a supervising analyst and on the faculty at The William Alanson White Institute, has led a Process Group for Orthodox women rabbis-in-training for several years, and has written and presented on various topics relating to the role of grief and mourning in the creation of something new.

She has been writing and studying poetry for many years. *Wellspring* is her first collection. She is a mother of two grown children and lives with her husband in NYC.

www.ingramcontent.com/pod-product-compliance
Lightning Source LLC
Chambersburg PA
CBHW022047080426
42734CB00009B/1276